THE DARK HI[STORY OF] AMERICA'S OLD WEST

THE DARK HISTORY OF

AMERICA'S OLD WEST

Sean Callery

mc Marshall Cavendish
Benchmark
New York

Published by Marshall Cavendish Benchmark
An imprint of Marshall Cavendish Corporation

Website: www.marshallcavendish.us

Other Marshall Cavendish Offices:
Marshall Cavendish International (Asia) Private Limited, 1 New Industrial Road, Singapore 536196 • Marshall Cavendish International (Thailand) Co Ltd. 253 Asoke, 12th Flr, Sukhumvit 21 Road, Klongtoey Nua, Wattana, Bangkok 10110, Thailand • Marshall Cavendish (Malaysia) Sdn Bhd, Times Subang, Lot 46, Subang Hi-Tech Industrial Park, Batu Tiga, 40000 Shah Alam, Selangor Darul Ehsan, Malaysia

Library of Congress Cataloging-in-Publication Data

Callery, Sean.
The dark history of America's old West / by Sean Callery.
p. cm.—(Dark histories)
Summary: "A collection of dark deeds from America's old West"—Provided by publisher.
Includes bibliographical references and index.
ISBN 978-1-60870-086-8
1. West (U.S.)—History—19th century—Juvenile literature. 2. Pioneers—West (U.S.)—History—19th century—Juvenile literature. 3. Indians of North America—Wars—1866-1895—Juvenile literature. 4. Indians, Treatment of—North America—Juvenile literature. 5. Outlaws—West (U.S.)—History—19th century—Juvenile literature. I. Title.
F593.C255 2010
978'.02—dc22
2009041115

Editorial and design by
Amber Books Ltd
Bradley's Close
74–77 White Lion Street
London N1 9PF
United Kingdom
www.amberbooks.co.uk

Project Editor: Sarah Uttridge
Design: Andrew Easton
Picture Research: Terry Forshaw and Natascha Spargo

PICTURE CREDITS:
FRONT COVER: Background image: Stock.xchng; Left: Corbis/Brian A. Vikander; Right: Corbis/Images.com. BACK COVER: Corbis/Bettmann

AKG Images: 41 (North Wind Picture Archives); Alamy: 11 (North Wind Picture Archives), 21 (North Wind Picture Archives), 38 (North Wind Picture Archives); Art-Tech/Aerospace: 46, 48; Bridgeman Art Library: 19b (Bibliotheque Nationale, Paris), 42 (Look & Learn), 56 (Look & Learn), 57 (Peter Newark American Pictures), 59 (Look & Learn); Cody Images: 33; Corbis: 16 (Layne Kennedy), 22 (Bettmann), 23 (Bettmann), 24 (Bettmann), 26 (Bettmann), 28 (Poodles Rock), 39 (Joseph Sohm/Visions of America), 44 (Jonathan Blair), 45 (Bettmann), 52 (Bettmann); Dreamstime: 14b (Glenda Powers); Getty Images: 6 (Bridgeman Art Library), 18 (Bridgeman Art Library), 19t (Hulton Archive); Legends of America: 54, 55; Library of Congress: 12, 13, 14t, 15, 25, 32, 31, 37, 40, 47, 50, 58; Mary Evans Picture Library: 5, 30, 34, 49; Photos.com: Box background; TopFoto: 8 (Granger Collection), 10 (Granger Collection), 36 (Granger Collection)

Printed in China

135642

Contents

Chapter 1

Land Grabbers

The Wild West, also referred to as the American Old West, highlights a period of American history from the mid–1800s to the end of the nineteenth century. Covering the region west of the Mississippi River, the West was a seemingly endless stretch of open **territory** sparsely inhabited by American Indians and where bison numbering in the millions roamed freely. It did not take long, however, for American **settlers** to start making their way into this new frontier and leaving their mark.

The half century that makes up the Wild West was also a time of American expansion and opportunity when hundreds of thousands of settlers made their way westward. It was also a time in history that was marked by violence and tragedy.

Thousands of settlers headed west in the search for opportunity and a better life. The journey was filled with danger, including treacherous routes, bad weather, and hostile native tribes.

Ancient Homelands

Before the arrival of the settlers, America's west had been the homeland of **native peoples**. The U.S. government decided these native peoples had to be moved off of the land so settlers could establish it for themselves. The native peoples were offered new places to live (usually on land that the settlers did not want or considered worthless) through enforced arrangements known as treaties. However, if those lands proved to be of value, for example, by yielding gold or fresh water, the tribes were then forced to move on again.

During the nineteenth century about four hundred treaties were negotiated between the U.S. government and American-Indian tribes—but they didn't keep the peace and

American Indians from the Great Plains lived in tepees. These cone-shaped dwellings were often made of animal skin, usually from bison.

Dark Deals

Dark deals took place in North America for a long time. In the eighteenth and nineteenth centuries Britain, Spain, France, and Russia all grabbed parts of North America and passed them between one another like children trading baseball cards. In 1800 Spain secretly gave France the Louisiana Territory, named in honor of Louis XIV of France by French explorer René-Robert Cavelier in 1682. This vast chunk of land covered 828,000 square miles (2,147,000 square kilometers) and stretched from the Mississippi River west to the Rocky Mountains, and included the strategic port of New Orleans in Louisiana. Three years later the French sold it to the United States in the Louisiana Purchase to raise money for their war with the British.

the native peoples lost their ancient homelands. In the end, a series of wars destroyed the American-Indian way of life. It is a dark story of suffering and broken promises.

Hit and Run

The United States successfully fought Spain for control of Florida from 1813 to 1819, but the conflict led to tension between the Americans and the Seminole tribe who lived in the area. Over the next eighteen years the vastly outnumbered warriors used hit-and-run tactics in order to avoid fighting major battles with the U.S. army. They would **ambush** small groups, killing soldiers and grabbing supplies, and then race away before the army could respond. These "guerilla" tactics cost the United States $40 million—more than twice what the Louisiana Purchase had cost them.

In 1830 the U.S. government passed the Indian Removal Act. Land that once belonged to several Indian nations was now available for white settlers. By 1837 many tribes had been forced to move. They were promised new lands, but these were often unsuitable, populated by animals the tribes did not hunt, and with little land suitable for them to grow crops.

The Trail of Tears

A particularly dark event that took place was the forced march of the **Cherokee** in the winter of 1838. The journey is known as the Trail of Tears. About 15,000 Cherokee trekked roughly 1,200 miles (1,900 kilometers) in six months to Indian Territory (later Oklahoma and Arkansas), even though rival tribes already occupied some of the land.

The Trail of Tears was the result of the U.S. government's forceful removal of the Cherokee people from their ancestral lands in the Southeast.

About four thousand of these travelers died from starvation, thirst, disease, or exposure. In all, five tribes with 70,000 members were moved in this way during the 1830s.

The Grattan Massacre

On August 18, 1854, a member of the Brulé Lakota (**Sioux**) tribe shot a lame cow that was lagging behind the rest of a settler's herd on the Oregon Trail – the main overland route across the West. The owner, who was traveling on the trail nearby, complained about his animal being killed, but the local post commander didn't consider it worth following up.

However, his lieutenant, John Grattan, felt otherwise and led a group of thirty soldiers to arrest the cow killer. The Brulé tribe offered to pay for the loss in horses, but as the talks went on a shot was fired, possibly by accident. This sparked a shootout. Conquering Bear, the Brulé leader, was shot as he tried to stop the gunfire. In the battle that followed all thirty American soldiers were killed. The army wanted revenge. A year later, in response to this **massacre**, the army destroyed a Brulé village and its hundred-strong population of men, women, and children.

The Sand Creek Massacre

In 1851 the **Treaty** of Fort Laramie gave the Cheyenne and Arapaho tribes a large area of land, now in present-day Wyoming, Nebraska, and Colorado. After seven years, gold was discovered there. The U.S. government wanted to remove the native peoples there so the treaty was renegotiated. The tribes were to be given a new, but far smaller, reserve in eastern Colorado.

Not all the American Indians agreed with this and the arguments among them continued after they moved to their new lands. The tribes resented the settlers traveling across their territory to the gold fields, and in return the American Indians were accused of stealing. In May 1864 a group of soldiers discovered that the Cheyenne had set up a bison-hunting camp near the Smoky Hill River. In response, the soldiers shot Cheyenne chiefs. The Cheyenne took revenge but later agreed to come to a camp near Fort Lyon to try to reach an agreement.

Counting Coup

American Indians measured bravery through a scoring system called "counting coup." "Coup" is the French word for "hit." Killing someone from a distance with a bow and arrow earned the least points. More points were earned for a blow with the spear, hatchet, or best of all, the hand or the coup stick. Scores were recorded with notches in the stick or feathers in the headdress.

Over seven hundred soldiers were involved in the Sand Creek Massacre. More than a hundred Cheyenne were killed, many of them women and children.

Scalping

American Indians and frontiersmen would sometimes scalp their enemies, alive or dead. This is cutting a line through the skin on the top of the forehead and pulling off the hair and flesh. If the victim survived, their face would droop afterward. Some Indian warriors wore scalps as a sign of their strength in battle.

On the morning of November 29, 1864, the U.S. army attacked this camp, ignoring the American flag and a white flag flown to show peaceful intent. At least 150 Cheyenne, mostly women and children, were killed. Then the soldiers looted the site, cutting off parts of the dead bodies as souvenirs. As a result of this slaughter the Cheyenne trusted the white men even less and undertook many acts of revenge on soldiers and settlers.

The Long Walk of the Navajo

The year 1864 also saw the defeat of another tribe, the **Navajo**, in New Mexico. The Navajo and other tribes had been carrying out raids on settlers, and the government wanted to send them to a reservation at Bosque Redondo, near Fort Sumner in New Mexico, away from the settlers. Only four hundred of the ten thousand Navajo agreed to make the twenty-day walk and many of the others hid in their Canyon de Chelly homeland.

Colonel Kit Carson decided to starve them out of their homeland by destroying their orchards, crops, and livestock. In the spring of 1864 most of the Navajo gave in and began the 300-mile (480-km) trek to their new reservation. About two hundred died of cold and starvation on the journey. This journey is known as the Long Walk of the Navajo or the Long Walk to Bosque Redondo. It was a disaster even for those who survived the journey because the land didn't suit their way of life. Four years later the U.S. government recognized its mistake and allowed them back to their homeland.

Kit Carson led a war against the Navajo, destroying their crops, orchards, and livestock before forcing them onto the Long Walk.

Conflict in the Black Hills

Ten years later it was lumber and gold that led to another major battle between the American Indians and the U.S. army. New settlements in Missouri needed timber. There was a plentiful supply in the Black Hills, which could be floated down the Cheyenne River. Then gold was found there, too. But, as a government official pointed out, this was reservation land for the Lakota tribe. He was ignored.

Little Bighorn

When the Lakota refused to move, the army tried to force them and this set off the Great Sioux War of 1876–1877 (the Sioux people are made up of several tribes including the

The Battle of Little Bighorn was a disaster for the U.S. cavalry. Many soldiers were killed and their bodies cut up by Sitting Bull's warriors.

Lakota). Its most famous skirmish was the Battle of the Little Bighorn (also known as Custer's Last Stand).

The Lakota and Northern Cheyenne, led by Sitting Bull killed more than half of the 7th Cavalry Regiment of the U.S. army, including its famous leader George Custer. The American Indians released their bows with deadly accuracy and many soldiers fell, pierced by more than one arrow. Soldiers who tried to run away were chased and killed. Many of the dead and wounded had their skulls crushed by clubs. Seeing this, some soldiers shot themselves to avoid the suffering. In the Battle of the Little Bighorn, sixteen U.S. officers and 242 soldiers died.

In the end, after a winter with little food, the Sioux tribes had no choice but to leave the Black Hills and go to a new reservation. Crazy Horse, one

Crazy Horse fought for the survival of his Lakota tribe. His mountain memorial can be seen in South Dakota.

The Sioux Ghost Dance had a peaceful religious message but it frightened the white settlers and led to distrust and fighting.

of their leaders, was forced to give up his weapons and horses. But the army did not trust him and feared he would lead his people to new lands. On September 5, 1877, they arrested him and forced him into a guardhouse. There was a struggle. He was stabbed and died from his wounds.

Wounded Knee

The final dark deed was the massacre at Wounded Knee Creek, South Dakota, on December 28, 1890. Around this time the Sioux tribe had adopted a religious movement called the Ghost Dance. It foretold of a peaceful end to American expansion. The dance was a spiritual ritual, though some danced it to antagonize the white settlers who misinterpreted it as a dance in preparation for war.

Tensions were running high. The Sioux had been forced to new, unproductive lands in South Dakota, and were told to hand over their weapons. However, while they were doing so a shot was fired and suddenly the five hundred troops of the U.S. 7th Cavalry were firing into the Sioux at point-blank range. When the gun smoke lifted, 153 Lakota Sioux lay dead with another fifty wounded. Twenty-five soldiers died, mostly from friendly fire in the confusion. Twenty soldiers were later given Medals of Honor for their part in the slaughter.

Chapter 2

Plains Tragedy

It was not just humanity that suffered as the West was conquered. American Indians were all but wiped off of the Great Plains in the nineteenth century, but so were bison and pigeons.

The Great Plains, an enormous stretch of **prairie** and steppe, extends across the middle of the United States (it also reaches north into Canada and south into Mexico) between the Mississippi River and the Rocky Mountains. This prairie land covers about 2,000 miles (3,200 km) north to south and 500 miles (800 km) east to west.

The Great Plains stretch across the middle of the United States. The tribes who inhabited them were doomed by pioneer expansion.

The Great Plains

Early in the nineteenth century the Great Plains was called the Great American Desert. A government report said it was "unfit for human habitation." However, the U.S. government let the American Indians occupy it as reservation land in order to move them off more valuable farmland elsewhere.

Land of Bison

But the Great Plains had bison, also known as buffalo, which were a highly valuable resource for the American Indians. Estimates of the original number of bison living on the plains vary from 25 to 70 million. The American Indians would follow the giant herds as they grazed the grasses of the plains. They would settle in areas where they

Pioneers crossed the Great Plains in long wagon trains. Hauled by oxen and horses, covered wagons provided protection from the hostile weather.

The grasslands of the Great Plains were the perfect habitat for the American bison that wandered huge distances.

knew the bison would pass by at certain times of the year and await their arrival. They only killed what they needed for food and hides and made tools from the bones. No part of the animal was wasted. Some tribes also settled long enough to grow crops every year on the Great Plains.

During the Civil War (1861–1865) the native peoples had lived peacefully on the Great Plains. However, in 1864, Major John Chivington, a militia officer from Colorado, attacked a peaceful village of Arapahos and Southern Cheyenne at Sand

The Choctaw tribe were one of the original people of the Southeast. They were forced from their lands on the Trail of Tears march.

The Big Kill

The pace of the bison killing was astonishing. It was only in 1880 that white hunters really took an interest in the northern herds. In 1882 there were five thousand white hunters and skinners at work on the plains. Skilled hunters could kill one hundred bison a day. By the end of the following year, there were hardly any bison left.

When trains began traveling across the Great Plains in 1869 the railroad operators didn't like bison either. A herd sheltering near the tracks could hold up a train for days. It became a common sport to shoot bison from a passing train. Another reason for killing bison was to take the hides, but many more were killed than were needed. Of the million a year that were slaughtered, about four out of every five were left to rot. Huge piles of bones were collected to be ground up for fertilizer.

The U.S. government encouraged bison hunting because it made more land available for raising cattle. It also meant that fewer bison equaled fewer troublesome tribes. By the beginning of the 1880s raids by the American Indians were almost over.

Creek in Colorado, killing more than 150 people. The attack set off a larger war with the native peoples. To subdue them, the U.S. government decided to kill off all the bison so that the American Indians would lose a primary source of food and either starve to death or be forced to move onto reservations.

This was a plan devised by General Philip Sheridan who wrote of the hunters, "Let them kill, skin, and sell until the buffalo is exterminated." He combined this destruction of the American-Indian food source with attacks on their winter quarters, killing all who refused to leave, including women and children. It is said that a Comanche chief once said to him, "Me Tosawi. Me good Indian." Sheridan replied, "The only good Indians I ever saw were dead."

Pigeon Feed

North America was once home to 3 to 5 billion passenger pigeon. The birds flew in flocks one mile (1.6 km) wide and 300 miles (500 km) long. Yet there were hardly any left by the end of the century because they had been killed to feed slaves.

Although banned in the northern states, slavery continued in the southern states, which relied on slave labor to work the tobacco, rice, and cotton plantations. By 1860 there were 4 million slaves working on these plantations in terrible conditions. Their owners fed them

Manifest Destiny

The government justified its actions with a very simple belief backed by the phrase "**Manifest Destiny.**" Americans believed that God wanted the United States to stretch from the Atlantic to the Pacific coasts, and therefore nothing and no one should stop this expansion.

inexpensive food such as pigeon meat. Huge numbers of the birds were trapped in nets, often attracted by a decoy that had been tied to a pole. Hunters crushed the birds' heads with their fingers and sold them for two cents a pair. There were hardly any passenger pigeons left by the middle of 1890s.

Destroying an Ancient Way of Life

Although there were plenty of killings and wrongdoing on both sides, the greatest dark deed was the destruction of the American-Indian way of life. American Indians were accustomed to following the bison herds and antelope. They understood nature and how to survive by living off of the land, but they lost

Flocks of passenger pigeons once filled the skies of North America but by the end of the century they were almost extinct.

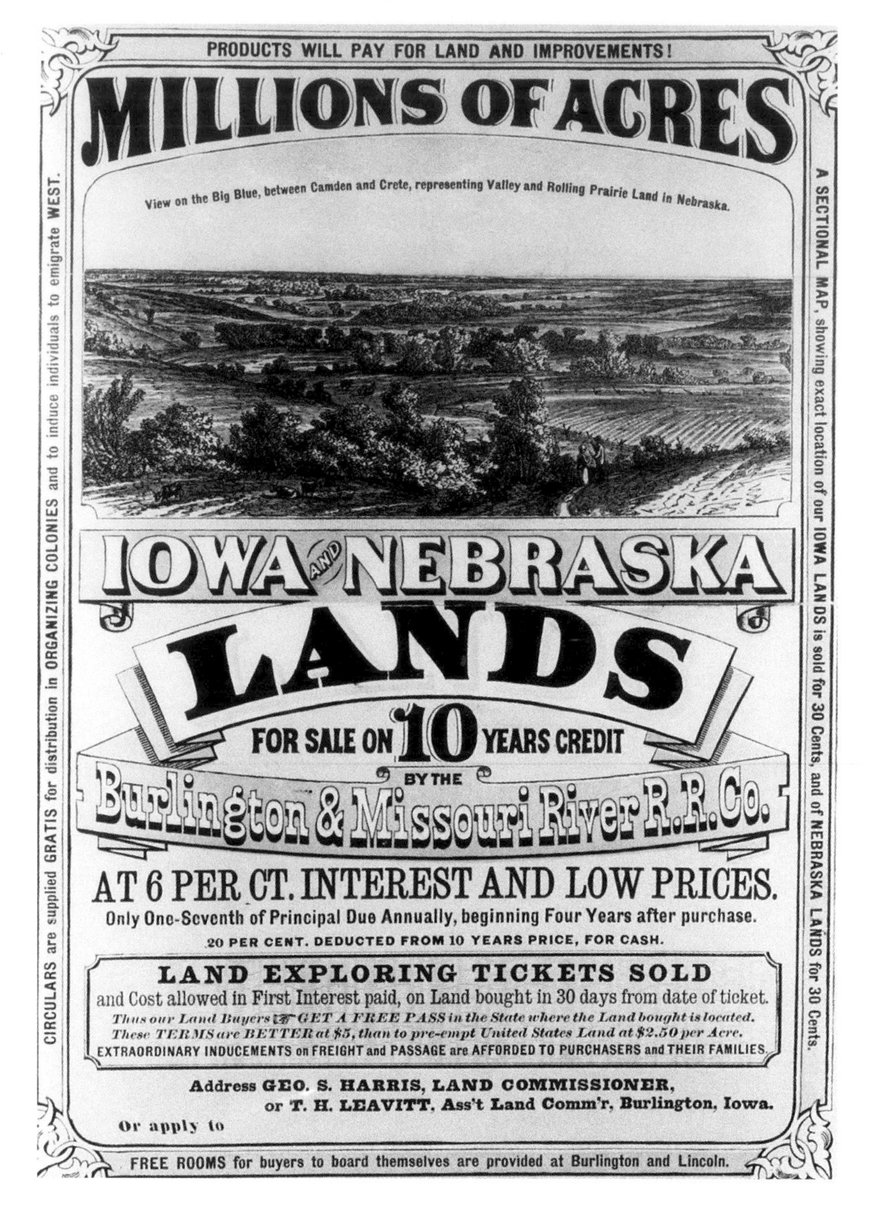

Newspapers and flyers throughout the East Coast advertised the sale of cheap land in the West.

these territories through treaties. If a treaty was not legal because too few leaders signed it, it was called an "agreement" and imposed anyway. Shut inside their reservations the American Indians became dependent on the U.S. government for food and supplies.

Free Land

The Homestead Act of 1862 was another major blow to the American Indians of the Great Plains. This act allowed any settler to mark out 160 acres (65 hectares) of uncultivated land for himself. If the settler stayed on the land for five years the land was his for free. Hundreds of thousands of people took up the offer. However, much of the land the settlers marked out for themselves had been set aside for American-Indian reservations. But life was tough on the new farms because water was scarce on the Great Plains. With their centuries of knowledge, the American Indians had learned other ways to survive successfully on the Great Plains. However, they had been thrown off or murdered to enable white settlers to try and farm it.

Some settlers on the Great Plains raised cattle because they could survive successfully there, much as the bison did. However, cattle farmers would try to find ways to keep their

Life on the open range was tough. There were many dangers and always the risk of losing the herd in a stampede.

herd on public lands for free while preventing their competitors from using it. Or they would get their cowboys to buy land and then transfer it to them. This avoided rules that were meant to limit how much land one individual could take.

Brand New Crime

Cattle rustling was a big problem. Because the cattle roamed over vast areas it wasn't possible to watch over all of them all of the time. So robber cowboys would round them up and lead them to their own lands. One way to recover stolen cattle was to brand them with an identifying mark, such as letters or symbols that showed who owned them. But this provided another opportunity for crime. The design had to be simple, often using square-, triangle-, and diamond-shaped irons. However, it was easy to change the symbol. For example it only takes a little effort to change a "*C*" to an "*O*," or a "*P*" to a "*B*." Cattle **rustlers** would do this to conceal the theft.

Range Wars

Access to water and disputes over grazing rights led to range wars. Farmers and ranchers fought for land and rights. They battled over fencing, because those who fenced off their property blocked cattle trails and routes to waterholes.

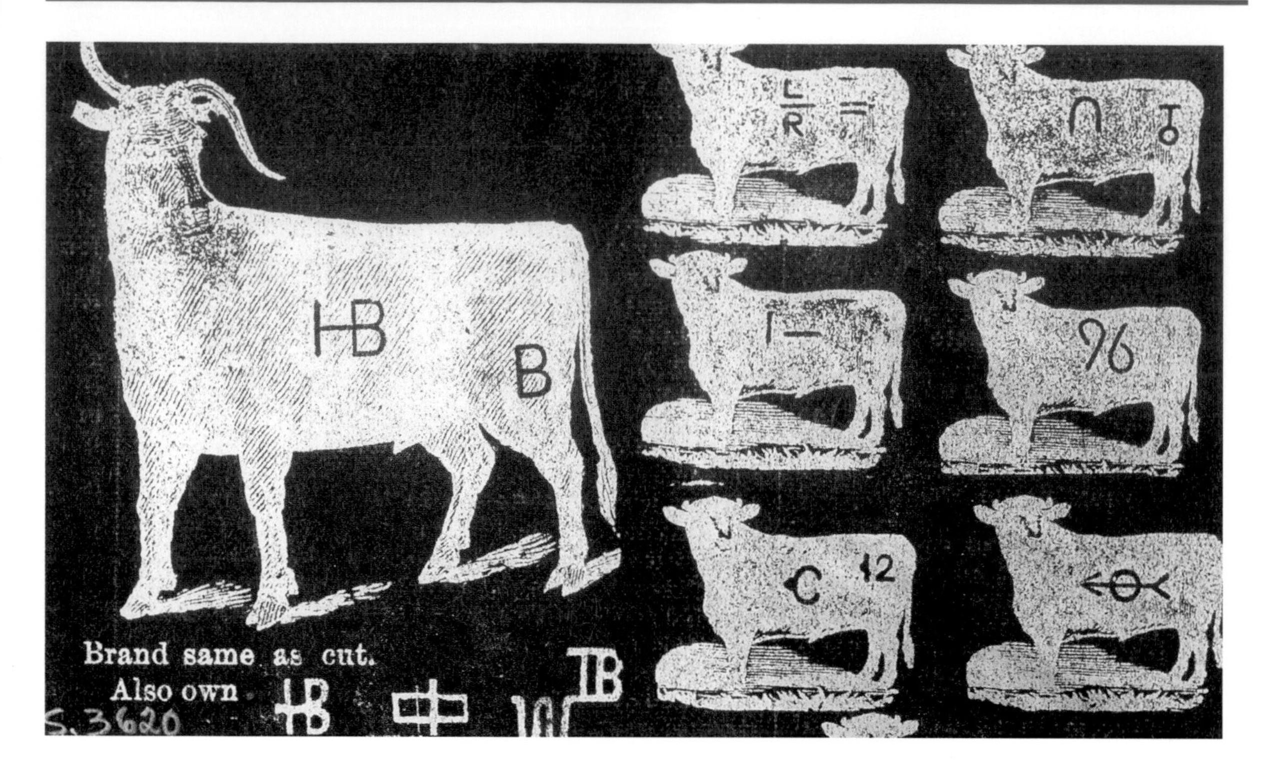

Cattle brands were meant to be unique and to help identify the owner, but it was common for stolen livestock to be "re-branded" with altered designs.

Double Prices

Cattle were herded across huge distances to be sold and slaughtered for their meat. This provided another opportunity for the unscrupulous trader to get paid twice over. Payment was per head of cattle. This was calculated by counting each cow as it passed. But corrupt cowboys had a simple trick of bringing the herd around in a circle so that each animal passed the counting point more than once, doubling the value of the herd.

The Johnson County War in April 1892 was one of the biggest range wars started with rival ranchers in Wyoming. It began with **vigilante** killings as people from the larger ranches killed a number of suspected cattle rustlers. Some were most likely innocent, but were from smaller ranches. Hired killers, a **sheriff**'s **posse**, and eventually the U.S. cavalry became involved.

Then the Wyoming Stock Growers Association hired gunmen from Texas to do a bigger job. They were paid five dollars a day and given a list of seventy targets to kill (for a bonus of fifty dollars a head), plus a number of ranch houses to be burned down.

They set to work and besieged a ranch, gunning down its occupants as they tried to escape. Nate Champion kept a diary of the attack. He wrote, "They have just got through shelling the house like hail. I heard them splitting wood. I guess they are going to fire the house tonight. I think I will make a break when night comes, if alive." When he ran from the back door bullets from four different guns hit him. A note was pinned to his chest saying, "Cattle Thieves Beware."

A sheriff's posse was called and they chased the killers who, in turn, took refuge in a log barn. Three of them were killed as they tried to escape. Eventually the 6th Cavalry arrived to save them from the lawmen.

But not everybody stopped on the Great Plains. Many more were just passing through on one of the toughest journeys of the nineteenth century.

Ranching was a massive industry. Cattle were herded across the country to where their meat could be sold for the best price.

Chapter 3

From Trails to Trains

The Oregon Trail was one of the main routes **migrants** used to travel as they journeyed westward. These travelers began their trip from locations on the Missouri River such as Independence, Missouri, all the way to present-day Oregon. The 2,000-mile (3,200-km) journey took settlers west through the Great Plains, a land that was also referred to as the Prairie Ocean or the Great American Desert. The journey lasted four to six months. Their covered wagons were sometimes called prairie schooners because they looked like ships sailing at sea. Once the settlers arrived in Oregon Territory (now Idaho, Oregon, and Washington) they could claim land to farm.

The journey westward was long and hard. Pioneers spent most of the day traveling the numerous—and often treacherous—trails. The evenings were a time to relax and unwind.

Dangerous Journeys

Traveling along the wagon trail was a long, tough journey. There were muddy tracks, dangerous rivers, food and water shortages, the threat of fire, terrible diseases, and the danger of attack from wild animals and American Indians. However, starting in the late 1830s hundreds of thousands of pioneers chose to take the trail to start a new life.

Drowning

There were many hazards along the way, but one common danger was crossing rivers and creeks. Wagons often got stuck in the soft mud of the riverbeds. Sometimes whole wagons

Water crossings were a regular hazard on the trail. Deep rivers had strong currents that could sweep away people and their possessions.

Hidden Killer

Scurvy, a disease caused by the poor diet of many migrants, was a hidden killer along the trail. The travelers ate mainly flour-based foods and salted pork. These foods are very low in vitamin C. Scurvy sufferers would grow pale, get spots on their skin (mostly on the legs and thighs), then their teeth would fall out, and their joints would seize up.

and their precious cargo would become caught in the swift current and float downstream to be smashed onto rocks. As the family struggled to push the wagons across the river, they would leave their youngest, most helpless children in the safety of the wagon. There are stories of wagons that overturned in churning whirlpools, taking babies and toddlers to a watery grave.

Diseases and other Dangers

Drowning was only one of the major risks posed on the trail. The biggest killers were diseases such as smallpox, typhoid, and cholera. However, there were other dangers, including freezing to death during the brutally cold winters. Accidents were also very common. Children and adults could easily slip while getting in or out of a moving wagon and fall under the wheels to be crushed to death or badly injured. Firearm accidents were another major cause of death, but guns were needed to ward off attacks by American Indians, especially if people strayed off the trail. The livestock that often accompanied the wagon trains was the cause of more danger. If a herd of cattle stampeded, you had to move fast to get out of the way. Unfortunately, not everybody managed to escape their deadly trample.

It is hard to say how many migrants died on the trail. Many were often buried in unmarked graves along the way. However, it is estimated that of the 400,000 pioneers on the trail, 16,000 never made it.

Cattle Drives

Vast herds of cattle were driven across the plains to be sold for their meat in the expanding cities. Life was tough for the cowboys on the trail. They rode for fourteen hours a day and had to keep watch on the cattle through the night. They could be fined for drinking, gambling, fighting, and swearing. It was hot and dusty on the trail during the day, but the

Stampedes

It didn't take much to start a **stampede**. A snap of a twig or a clap of thunder would set the whole herd running wild. The cowboys would have to ride to the front of the stampede to stop it. It was easy to slip or fall and that meant instant death by being crushed under the cattle's hooves.

nights were very cold and they only had blankets for keeping warm at night. If a cowboy got sick or had an accident, there was little help for him. It was not a job for life and few cowboys lasted more than seven years.

The Iron Path

Building a railroad linking the eastern and western United States was a massive achievement. The "**Iron Path**" covered 1,776 miles (2,860 km) of rugged wilderness from Omaha, Nebraska, to Sacramento, California, linking with existing tracks to join the Pacific and Atlantic coasts. But dark deeds were done to raise money to build it.

The railroad was built after the U.S. government passed the Pacific Railroad Act in 1862. The act guaranteed payment for every mile of track laid plus generous amounts

Swift but Unpleasant

The quickest way to travel across the middle of the United States was by stagecoach. It took about twenty-two days to travel the Oregon Trail, but it probably took the same length of time to recover from the trip.

Passengers were squeezed three to a bench, with about 15 inches (38 centimeters) of seat each as the stagecoach bounced along rough roads. The coach stopped every 12 miles (20 km) or so only to change mules. It kept going night and day as passengers slept in their seats, their knees bashing against those of their fellow travelers. It was boiling hot during the day, freezing cold at night, and always dusty. The coaches overturned frequently on the bumpy roads and they were particularly vulnerable to robberies and attack by American Indians.

of land—provided the whole job was done by 1876. Building the railroad was going to cost a lot of money. Some businessmen took this as an opportunity to swindle investors and the government. By raising funds for construction, paying bribes, and trading in stocks and bonds, businessmen gathered huge personal fortunes while their companies had little value. In a major crisis known as the **Panic of 1873** (when the American economy was badly damaged and banks went bust and factories closed) 89 out of the 364 railroad companies went out of business.

In another scam, a firm called Credit Mobilier charged Union Pacific too much money for carrying out track work. Congressman Oakes Ames was asked to deal with the problem. Instead, he put his brother in charge of Union Pacific, became president of Credit Mobilier himself, and sold stock at a price greatly below the true value to fellow congressmen.

Building the railroad was hard. The work was tough and there were dangers from the terrain, the weather, and the risk of attack by local tribes.

When his actions were later discovered, he earned the nickname "Hoax Ames."

Back Breaking

The railroad was built from east and west. The Union Pacific headed west using a labor force of Irishmen and army veterans. The Central Pacific, which headed eastward, had a workforce that was mainly local but included people of Chinese descent. The Central Pacific track had to cross the Sierra Nevada Mountains, which involved cutting through a peak 7,000 feet (2,100 meters) high. The Chinese workers were not well treated and were given the worst jobs until the bosses realized that they did an excellent job.

It was incredibly hard work to get the ground ready. Each iron rail weighed 700 pounds (320 kilograms) and needed five men to lift. They used basic tools such as plows, scrapers, picks, axes, chisels, and sledgehammers to hack away at the rock. In some places they had to blast it out of the way, using gunpowder, **dynamite**, or **nitroglycerine**. Mistakes could, and did, cost lives.

Swing and Blast

There are remarkable tales of Chinese workers developing a system of hanging by ropes in wicker baskets as they drilled holes into the rock and inserted dynamite, swinging out of the way just before the rock was blasted apart. These laborers carried out incredibly difficult jobs living and working in very tough conditions.

Brutal Conditions

The railroad workers labored through the harsh winters and some froze to death. Their bodies were found when the snows thawed, still clutching their picks or shovels. It is known that 100 to 150 workers died during the construction of the railroad.

The historic moment on May 10, 1869, when the two ends of the first transcontinental railway line were connected.

Some people believe the figure is far higher because deaths were not properly reported and bodies were quickly buried by the side of the tracks.

Many Accidents

The two railroad lines met at Promontory Summit on May 10, 1869. Three more transcontinental lines opened by 1883. This meant the journey across the nation was cut from at least four months to about a week. But the work had been done in a great rush. Some of the tracks had not been weighed down properly with rock, some bridges were flimsy, and the ties were sometimes of poor quality. This caused many accidents and nearly 12,000 passengers and workers died over the next forty years. But the danger of the railroads was nothing compared to the horrors of the gold mines.

Chapter 4

Yellow Metal Madness

The story of the search for gold is a dark tale of greed and fear. American-Indian medicine man Black Elk called gold "the yellow metal that drives white men crazy." Indeed, the discovery of gold in the Wild West led to insane behavior. Men would rush to the hills, ignoring any question of who owned the land where these precious nuggets might be found. Towns were built in the middle of nowhere, and were just as quickly abandoned with the next rumor of a "get-rich-quick" site. In between there was suffering, arguments, fights, and killings.

Gold brought riches for some and trouble for many. Death struck in many of the lawless gold camps through disease, poverty, or fighting.

Free For All

In 1848 James Marshall was setting up a sawmill for John Sutter on the American River in Coloma, California. He needed to widen a ditch where the water flowed from the machine. On the morning of January 24, he noticed some shiny pieces of rock in the water. It was gold.

For the first year or so it was mostly local people who came in search of gold, and many found it. Six months of backbreaking searching could yield gold worth six years' wages. California was not even a state at this time so there was no government, taxes, and private property: it was a free-for-all. Word spread, not just across the United States, but around the globe.

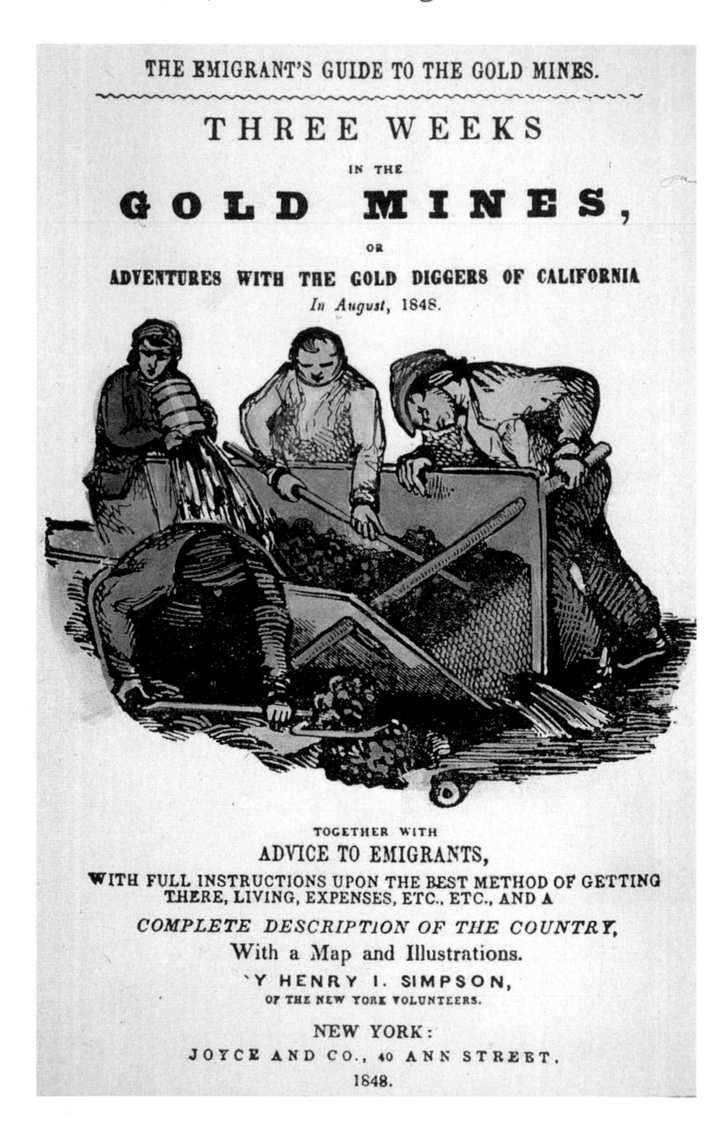
THE EMIGRANT'S GUIDE TO THE GOLD MINES.

THREE WEEKS

IN THE

GOLD MINES,

OR

ADVENTURES WITH THE GOLD DIGGERS OF CALIFORNIA

In August, 1848.

TOGETHER WITH

ADVICE TO EMIGRANTS,

WITH FULL INSTRUCTIONS UPON THE BEST METHOD OF GETTING THERE, LIVING, EXPENSES, ETC., ETC., AND A

COMPLETE DESCRIPTION OF THE COUNTRY,

With a Map and Illustrations.

`Y HENRY I. SIMPSON,

OF THE NEW YORK VOLUNTEERS.

NEW YORK:

JOYCE AND CO., 40 ANN STREET.

1848.

Abandon Ship!

The population of California, excluding American Indians, was 14,000 when Marshall spotted those shiny flecks in the water. By the end of 1852 it had soared to more than 250,000. People came from all over the world, crossing the oceans to the port of San Francisco and trekking to the hills in the hope of striking it rich. Some ships were abandoned without crews in the port as their sailors left to seek riches.

Most of them had no idea how to find gold. They just packed a

News of gold rushes spread fast and led to the arrival of thousands of prospectors. Many of them had little idea of how to find gold.

After the discovery of gold in 1848, Butte, California, became an established mining community.

few basic supplies, a pick, and a shovel, and headed for the tents and log cabins of the gold camps that sprang up north and south of the river. Some were lucky. In 1848 the take was $10 million, the next year it was more than four times that, and the figures for 1851 and 1852 were $75 million and $81 million. After this, however, the totals started to drop. But then other gold fields to dig were discovered, and gold rushes continued to take place in the Wild West throughout the second half of the nineteenth century.

Ruin

The two men who started the California gold rush were ruined by it. After gold was discovered in 1848 neither John Marshall nor the sawmill owner John Sutter could get anyone to work there because they were all off **panning** for gold. Eventually, aggressive prospectors forced Sutter off his land. He said, "By this sudden discover of gold, all my great plans were destroyed.... Instead of being rich, I am ruined." Sutter spent the rest of his life

Gold prospectors spent long hours each day sifting through riverbed soil in search of the precious metal.

trying to get his land back, but he failed and died in 1880. James Marshall died almost broke in 1885.

Panning for gold was tough. Called placer mining, the prospectors collected dirt from riverbeds and streambeds. They rinsed and sifted through the dirt looking for gold flecks, sometimes standing up to their waist in freezing water all day. But there was no place here for doctors to treat the sick, the few stores that there were charged gold-crazy high prices, and the miners had no way to keep their money safe apart from the threat of a gun. Theft was common.

Claim Jumping

A prospector could claim land just by working on it. In some regions each claim was only 10 feet (3 m) across. But people abandoned sites if they felt they weren't finding enough gold there. They would move to another claim in hopes of finding more. Then someone else would start working on the abandoned site. This was called **claim jumping**. And if the newcomer found gold, there would be a dispute about who owned it. With no laws or lawmen around, the argument often turned into a fight. It is estimated that as many as one in five of the thousands of prospectors who had headed into California to prospect for gold died, many of them violently.

Unfair Taxes

California had been part of Mexico until 1846 when the United States won it in a war. The gold rush attracted waves of Mexican prospectors back to their old lands. Many had worked

Tricksters

Land that was considered worthless was suddenly worth a fortune if gold was discovered in its rocks and soil. Some people known as tricksters, bought low-value land and then placed a few nuggets on the ground or even fired gold dust onto the hillside. Then they encouraged excited newcomers to pay high prices for the land. This trick of planting gold and then selling the diggings was called "salting a claim."

as miners and so knew how to find gold. This led to jealousy from the Americans and there were frequent fights. In April 1850 the newly established state of California started to tax foreign miners twenty dollars a month. It was mainly aimed at the Mexicans and caused resentment because it was so unfair.

A second foreign miner's tax was imposed in May 1852. This time it was aimed at the growing number of Chinese miners who were arriving after a serious crop failure in southern China left them starving and out of work. There were robberies and fights.

Settlements grew out of nothing and were then abandoned as the gold ran out, leaving a ghost town to haunt the landscape.

Some gold mining methods ruined the landscape leaving behind crumbling hillsides and rivers full of garbage.

Landscape Mayhem

Starting in 1853 a new way of loosening the soil to sift for gold was developed. **Hydraulic mining** used a powerful water hose to wash the dirt, soil, and silt. Prospectors needed money for the equipment and so needed backing from big businesses. But hydraulic mining had a terrible effect on the landscape, turning it into a series of massive molehills. The soil from crumbled hillsides choked up the rivers with sediment, and low-lying farms were flooded or buried in sand. Hydraulic mining was eventually banned in 1884, but some prospectors carried on in secret and damage to the landscape continued.

Shaft Mines

After most of the gold that lay on or near the surface was found, the search was on to find the veins of gold in the rocks farther below. In order to look for it, shaft mines were dug straight down into the ground. The most desperate newcomers, working in terrible conditions underground, manned these mines.

The mines stank of blasting powder, unwashed bodies, rotten timber, and human waste. Ventilation was poor so the air quality was low, causing headaches and dizziness. It was unbearably hot deep underground and many miners died from heatstroke. Other fatalities were caused by explosions and cave-ins.

More Rushes

The Californian gold rush was the first of many. Soon gold was discovered in Colorado, Utah, Arizona, New Mexico, Idaho, Montana, and South Dakota. If the precious metal was found on Indian reservations, land treaties were "renegotiated" to remove the native peoples living there and allow for mining. However, this usually happened after prospectors had occupied the territory and had started digging anyway.

Gold towns attracted crooks, bandits, professional gamblers, and others eager to grab their share of riches without actually doing any mining. There were also the so-called bedroll killers, who crept up on sleeping or drunk prospectors and slashed their throats or caved in their skulls and then stole their gold. The Wild West was entering a truly lawless stage.

The saloon in a gold town was a dangerous place to be. You could be robbed, conned, or killed with little chance of the law being enforced.

Chapter 5

Violence and Vigilantes

The West was a land of opportunity for many law-abiding settlers who wanted to lead a new life. Others saw their opportunities by cheating settlers, stealing horses, robbing banks, ambushing stagecoaches, and raiding trains. Some of these **outlaws** became famous for their exploits. Most died violently, murdered by an angry mob that had taken the law into their own hands.

It was an exciting time for those who wanted to build a new life but also a frightening time, where there was the risk of violence at any opportunity.

Billy the Kid was just another dangerous outlaw during his short life. After he died, he became a popular hero and his name is still famous today.

Tough as Old Boots

The story of George Parrot illustrates how outlaws worked and how gruesome their fate often was. He was a bandit who was "tough as an old pair of boots," and, in fact, he was turned into a pair of shoes.

Known as Big Nose George, Parrot spent his life as a horse thief and highwayman in the 1870s. He was most attracted to the greater rewards offered by railroad crime. By August 16, 1878, he was part of a gang in Wyoming that bent railroad tracks so that any train traveling on them would be forced to stop in open country. The passengers stranded on the train in the middle of nowhere were then robbed.

However, Parrot and the gang were spotted, so they retreated to their camp at Rattlesnake Canyon near Elk Mountain. As two lawmen came across the camp, the robbers sprang up from their hiding place and shot them dead. Now the gang had a reward of $10,000 on their heads.

Big Nose George started out as a highwayman, stopping stagecoaches to rob the passengers.

The Gentleman Robber

Charles Bolles was a famous stagecoach robber in northern California and southern Oregon in the 1870s and 1880s. Known as Black Bart, a name probably taken from a character in a comic book, he concealed his true identity by covering his face beneath a sack with cut-out eyeholes.

He only robbed stagecoaches run by the Wells Fargo company, against whom he seemed to have a grudge. He sometimes refused to take the terrified passengers' jewels, demanding only the safe box. Black Bart was always polite, saying "Please thrown down the box," although admittedly his request was always backed up by a raised shotgun. He was eventually caught when he left a laundry ticket behind as he escaped.

Way Out

Later, Big Nose George was heard boasting about the killings in Miles City, Montana. The sherriff caught him and put him on a train back to Wyoming. There he was found guilty and sentenced to be hung. But Big Nose George didn't want to swing. On the evening of March 22, 1881, he used a pocketknife and a piece of sandstone to file off the iron shackles on his ankles. He hid in the bathroom and leapt out at his jailer, Robert Rankin. He hit him so hard with the shackles that the blow fractured Rankin's skull and the jailer cried out, alerting his wife Rosa. She appeared holding a pistol and forced George back into his cell.

The locals decided enough was enough and they dragged Big Nose George from his cell and hanged him in the street in front of a crowd of two hundred people. The rope broke as George struggled and it took three attempts before the outlaw swung lifeless from a telegraph pole.

Jesse James rarely robbed train passengers. He preferred to take the valuables from the safe in the baggage car.

Brain Test

No family came to claim the body, so Dr. John Osborne decided to see if criminal brains were different from those of the law-abiding. He sawed off the top of George's skull and gave it to his medical assistant, Lillian Heath (who went on to become the first female doctor in Wyoming). She used the piece of skull for years as an ashtray and a doorstop. Then they made a death mask of George's face. The big nose that had inspired his nickname came up beautifully, but the ears were missing. They had worn away as the criminal wriggled on the **lynching** rope.

Osborne then removed the outlaw's skin and made it into a pair of shoes. The rest of the body was put into a whiskey barrel filled with salt solution to preserve it. This grisly container was found in May 1950 with George's bones and sawn-off skull still inside. Lilian Heath supplied the missing piece of skull, confirming the remains were those of Big Nose George.

Just a Hood, not Robin Hood

A famous outlaw called Jesse James had a reputation as a "Robin Hood" who robbed the rich to help the poor. But in fact he was just a common criminal who kept all his loot.

Jesse James and his brother Frank fought as Confederates in the Civil War and were involved in massacres of wounded or captured Union troops. After the war, starting in 1866, both were part of the James-Younger Gang, which committed twenty-six holdups. They killed at least seventeen men, some just bystanders who were tragically in the wrong place at the wrong time. The crime spree of the James-Younger Gang carried on for fifteen years.

Jesse James became a famous outlaw. His name appeared on posters like this, advertising a theater show where his hold-ups were acted out.

Hero Coverage

Jesse became famous after his gang robbed a Missouri bank in December 1869. One member of the gang, probably Jesse, shot the cashier because he wrongly thought the man had once killed a valued army colleague. Then the gang made a daring escape. Newspapers picked up on the incident and started to publish stories about the daredevil gang and its snappily dressed leader, Jesse. The papers portrayed him as a sort of hero who robbed companies and not people.

This image was strengthened in 1873 when the gang derailed and robbed their first train, in Adair, Iowa. However, the train driver was another innocent victim, killed when the engine overturned.

Betrayal

A botched bank raid on the First National Bank of Northfield, Minnesota, on September 7, 1876 left two bandits dead and only Frank and Jesse avoided capture. However, the gang

Sympathy for the Devil

One reason people felt sympathetic toward Jesse James was because of a failed attempt to catch him that went tragically wrong. In 1875 agents from the Pinkerton detective firm attacked the James family farm in Missouri. They tried to lure the brothers out by throwing a smoke bomb into the house. Jesse's younger stepbrother Archie thought it was a stick and threw it on the fire where it exploded. The blast killed him and injured their mother so badly she later lost an arm. Frank and Jesse weren't even home at the time.

was finished. Frank settled down but Jesse carried on with a new band of outlaws. His story ends in 1882 when one of them betrayed him for the $5,000 reward, dead or alive, that had been placed on his head.

Bob Ford and his brother Charley were in Jesse's house on the morning of April 3, 1882, planning a robbery. Jesse was suspicious of the brothers and kept his gun close by. But when Jesse temporarily dropped his guard and got up on a chair to adjust a picture Bob seized his chance, leapt at him, and shot him in the back of the head. In the space of a few hours the Ford brothers were charged with murder, sentenced to death, and pardoned, which suggested the authorities approved of the killing.

PROCLAMATION
OF THE
GOVERNOR OF MISSOURI!

REWARDS
FOR THE ARREST OF
Express and Train Robbers.

STATE OF MISSOURI,
EXECUTIVE DEPARTMENT.

WHEREAS, It has been made known to me, as the Governor of the State of Missouri, that certain parties, whose names are to me unknown, have confederated and banded themselves together for the purpose of committing robberies and other depredations within this State; and

WHEREAS, Said parties did, on or about the Eighth day of October, 1879, stop a train near Glendale, in the county of Jackson, in said State, and, with force and violence, take, steal and carry away the money and other express matter being carried thereon; and

WHEREAS, On the fifteenth day of July 1881, said parties and their confederates did stop a train upon the line of the Chicago, Rock Island and Pacific Railroad, near Winston, in the County of Daviess, in said State, and, with force and violence, take, steal, and carry away the money and other express matter being carried thereon; and, in perpetration of the robbery last aforesaid, the parties engaged therein did kill and murder one WILLIAM WESTFALL, the conductor of the train, together with one JOHN McCULLOCH, who was at the time in the employ of said company, then on said train; and

WHEREAS, FRANK JAMES and JESSE W. JAMES stand indicted in the Circuit Court of said Daviess County, for the murder of JOHN W SHEETS, and the parties engaged in the robberies and murders aforesaid have fled from justice and have absconded and secreted themselves:

NOW, THEREFORE, in consideration of the premises, and in lieu of all other rewards heretofore offered for the arrest or conviction of the parties aforesaid, or either of them, by any person or corporation, I, THOMAS T. CRITTENDEN, Governor of the State of Missouri, do hereby offer a reward of five thousand dollars ($5,000.00) for the arrest and conviction of each person participating in either of the robberies or murders aforesaid, excepting the said FRANK JAMES and JESSE W. JAMES; and for the arrest and delivery of said

FRANK JAMES and JESSE W. JAMES,

and each or either of them, to the sheriff of said Daviess County, I hereby offer a reward of five thousand dollars, ($5,000.00,) and for the conviction of either of the parties last aforesaid of participation in either of the murders or robberies above mentioned, I hereby offer a further reward of five thousand dollars, ($5,000.00.)

IN TESTIMONY WHEREOF, I have hereunto set my hand and caused to be affixed the Great Seal of the State of Missouri. Done at the City of Jefferson on this 28th day of July, A. D. 1881.

[SEAL.]

THOS. T. CRITTENDEN.

By the Governor:
MICH'L K. McGRATH, Sec'y of State.

The rewards paid for capturing outlaws kept most lawmen more interested in arresting criminals alive, rather than shooting them dead.

The Outlaw Queen

Belle Starr grew up with members of the James-Younger Gang and became hooked on living the life of an outlaw. She was one of the few women bandits, robbing banks and stagecoaches, earning the title of the "outlaw queen." She used to ride sidesaddle dressed in a black velvet riding habit and a feathered hat, carrying a pistol on each hip—she was a crack shot. She was killed on February 3, 1889. Sadly, she had few friends and there were many suspects, including her own husband and her son, who she had beaten for mistreating her horse. No one was ever charged with her murder.

Bob toured with a stage show telling the story of the killing. He was shot dead ten years later.

Brandy Head

In the 1850s Joaquin Murrieta came from Mexico with his family to California in search of gold. Faced with the tax on foreign miners and kicked off his land, he turned to crime and led an outlaw gang called The Five Joaquins. They are said to have killed nineteen people including three lawmen, and to have stolen more than $100,000 as well as one hundred horses. With a price of $5,000 on his head, Joaquin was hunted down and killed in 1853. His head was kept in a jar of brandy that was taken around the country. People were charged one dollar to view it. Depending on your point of view he was either a Mexican patriot, or a vicious desperado.

Chapter 6

Shoot First, Ask Questions Later

Throughout much of the Wild West, guns were used to settle arguments. In the gold town of Deadwood, South Dakota, in the 1870s, the homicide rate ran at more than one a day. Such towns were often built illegally and so did not have official **marshals** to enforce the law.

Most of the people were hard-working pioneers who wanted law and order. In many mining settlements, cow towns, and farming communities, people took the law into their own hands, developing their own system of trial and punishment. However, the age of the outlaws and do-it-yourself law enforcement was to be brought to an end by a new breed in the Wild West—the lawman.

William F. Cody, better known as Buffalo Bill, was a soldier and bison hunter. He made a fortune by organizing shows with cowboy themes that included shooting displays and attacks on wagon trains.

Vigilantes and Lawmen

Until the lawmen were brought in, trials were held in public with local people forming the jury to decide guilt. This meant trials were sometimes unfair. Those accused of wrongdoing could be convicted by the shouts of the crowd. But this was unjust because the outcome often depended on the popularity of the accused with the mob, not their guilt or innocence. Minority groups such as Mexicans or Chinese were more likely to be lynched by the mob than white Americans and Europeans. Many innocent people were killed as well as many criminals.

Sometimes there was no trial at all. The "vigilance committee" would put on masks, ride out, and grab the criminals. Punishments included whipping, banishment from the town or, most commonly, lynching, which meant being strung up from a tree or telegraph pole. However, states began to impose their laws through a new type of person in the form of the lawman.

An Outlaw Lawman

Lawmen were often ex-soldiers and even former outlaws. They had to be tough and some could not be relied upon to handle situations fairly. One of the roughest was

Sheriff Pat Garrett was made famous in 1881 for shooting Billy the Kid. Many people believed that Garrett killed the wanted outlaw in cold blood.

Steve Long, who used the role to rob. He had served in the Civil War and was a professional gunfighter before he became deputy marshal of Laramie City, Wyoming, in 1867. He was quick to use his gun, killing eight men in gunfights in his first two months. Long befriended two half-brothers Ace and Con Moyer and ran a saloon with them. This became the unofficial town court where the three men forced ranchers to hand over their land deeds and miners to surrender their claims.

If the ranchers refused, Long shot them and claimed they had pulled their gun first. He would place a rifle by the dead body as proof. Locals started calling the saloon the "Bucket of Blood" and a vigilante group was set up to stop the killings. Eventually they caught Long after he had been wounded while trying to rob a prospector who died shortly after. The vigilante mob stormed the saloon and strung up Long and the Moyer brothers. Long asked if he could remove his shoes, saying "My mother always said I'd die with my boots on." He proved her wrong. There is a photograph of the three hanging bodies and Long's feet are bare.

Killing Pole

Telegraph poles had a dark side. The invention of Morse code and the national system of telegraph lines meant messages could be sent in minutes rather than hours by horse or days by post. This meant that if a criminal was captured, even a long way away, local people would soon hear about it. If the people were angry enough, they'd halt the train bringing the accused back for trial and string him up from the nearest telegraph pole or tree.

No Gun

Not all lawmen were as eager to pull the trigger. One such lawman was Thomas J. Smith. On November 19, 1868, during his time as marshal of Bear City, Wyoming, a vigilante mob lynched a railroad employee suspected of murder. The accused man's friends were so angry they torched the town buildings and began a shootout. Smith bravely stood between the two groups and calmed them down until the army arrived, but not before sixteen people had been killed.

He gained the nickname "no gun marshal" because he banned guns in the towns he oversaw and settled disputes with his bare hands. This impressed the town of Abilene, which was so wild that when two policemen were hired as marshals they only lasted a few hours. They had been so horrified by the lawlessness there that they resigned before finishing their first day and climbed on the first train out of town.

Cruel Death

Smith became Abilene's lawman and was highly respected by most, but hated by others. He had survived two assassination attempts before he met a cruel death. On November 2, 1870, he went to arrest two farmers, Andrew McConnell and Moses Miles, who were accused of murder. A gunfight started and both McConnell and Smith were wounded when Miles struck Smith with his rifle butt, picked up an axe, and swung it. The blow took off the lawman's head.

Thomas J. Smith earned the nickname "no gun marshal" because he banned guns, preferring to settle arguments by talking.

Killer

Not every lawman was a true hero. The story of John Larn illustrates how wild life really was in Texas in the 1870s. Larn had had a troubled early life. As a young ranch hand in 1869 he murdered his employer in an argument over a horse. He fled to New Mexico and killed a local sheriff he thought was tracking him. He later killed two Mexicans and dumped their bodies in the Pecos River.

Gunfighters

Gunfighters (or gunslingers) were men who were highly skilled with a gun. They could be outlaws prepared to kill for money, bandits, or lawmen who administered justice. In the movies, gunfights are often shown with two men facing each other in the middle of the street, waiting for the first one to draw his weapon. In real life, gunfighters didn't take such risks and were more likely to ambush their victims.

Being a deputy marshal was a risky job. In Indian Territory (later Oklahoma) 103 deputies were killed between 1872 and 1896.

Then Larn settled down in Fort Griffin and joined a vigilante group called the Tin Hat Brigade, earning so much respect he ended up as Shackelford County sheriff in April 1876. That same month the brigade lynched a horse thief on a tree and left a pick and a shovel under the body in case anybody could be bothered to bury him. In the next six months two more horse thieves were shot and six hanged. Larn became a local hero.

Crime Solved

Larn set up a cattle business with his deputy. Local ranchers soon noticed an increase in cattle rustling, which surprised them considering how active the vigilante group was. But they soon realized that the only herd that wasn't being robbed was Larn's. Their hero marshal was the rustler.

Larn couldn't stay in the job and resigned as sheriff in 1877, and the following year was arrested for wounding a fellow rancher. Here was a chance for revenge. The local blacksmith shackled him to the floor of the jailhouse to prevent Larn's friends from rescuing him. Instead, vigilantes burst in to lynch him. When they found they couldn't get him out of his cell, they shot him where he was.

Wild Bill Hickok

One of the most famous gunslingers was Wild Bill Hickok. He was a crack shot and always carried a pair of silver-plated pistols with ivory handles. Hickok was involved in many

Wild Bill Hickok made his way west working as a stagecoach driver. He soon established his reputation as a lawman, gunfighter, and gambler.

Guest Trouble

When John Wesley Hardin came to stay in Abilene, people expected trouble. Hardin was the most dangerous gunslinger in the West and is thought to have murdered at least forty men. When he was kept awake by someone snoring in the next hotel room, the short-tempered gunslinger fired two shots through the wall. However, he quickly realized Hickok would not stand for that kind of behavior, so he stole a horse and left town still wearing his nightshirt.

shootouts and became famous because of newspaper articles about him that suggested he was heroic as a lawman.

Hickok enjoyed his fame and used to say, "Shoot first, ask questions later," to support his tough-guy image. In fact, he only killed five men, and one of those was a fellow lawman he shot by accident.

The story starts with a cowboy and a dog. On October 5, 1871, a cowboy called Phil Coe was celebrating the end of the cattle season when a stray dog tried to bite him, so he shot it. Hickok shouted at him that weapons weren't allowed in the town, and Coe pulled his gun. Hickok shot first, then heard a noise behind him, spun around, and shot again. The bullet killed his deputy who had been running up to assist Hickok. He had to resign as sheriff after that. In 1876, a rival at a card table shot Hickok dead.

When Bill Hickok sat with his back to the door, his enemy John (Jack) McCall seized his chance and shot him dead.

Calamity Jane

One of Bill Hickok's friends is probably now more famous than him. Calamity Jane was one of the best known characters of the frontier. She sometimes worked as a teamster (wagon driver) and bullwhacker (someone who keeps bulls and oxen moving)—both men's jobs, so she often dressed as a man. She was a crack shot and was known to shoot out the lights of a bar to announce her arrival.

The Gunfight at the O.K. Corral is the most famous gunfight in the history of the Wild West.

The Hot Springs Gunfight

The strangest gunfight was not between outlaws and lawmen, but between the police department and the sheriff's office—and more people died in it than in the famous gunfight at the O.K. Corral in Tombstone, Arizona, in 1881. But this was the Hot Springs Gunfight in Arkansas on March 16, 1899. Hot Springs was a gambling town and the lawmen were well-known for taking bribes. They argued over the money and went for their guns. By the end of the fight, five people lay dead.

Most of this new breed of lawmen preferred not to shoot because they were often paid bonuses for bringing criminals in alive rather than dead. By the close of the nineteenth century, the West was no longer Wild.

Glossary

Ambush
Where someone hides out of sight and then attacks by surprise.

Cherokee
A major American-Indian tribe in the Southeastern United States.

Claim Jumping
Working someone else's land. Claim jumping was common during the gold rush.

Counting Coup
Scoring system for the bravery of American-Indian warriors.

Dynamite
A high explosive material often used in the building of railroads, made with nitroglycerine.

Gold Rush
When many people came to a region in search of gold, triggered by a major find.

Great Plains
A series of huge plains stretching across the United States and Canada.

Hydraulic Mining
Mining with a pressurized water hose to wash away the soil.

Iron Path
The name for the railroad connecting the United States from East to West.

Lynching
Killing a suspected or convicted criminal, often by hanging.

Manifest Destiny
The belief that God wanted the United States to stretch from the Atlantic to the Pacific oceans.

Marshal
A law officer, similar to a sheriff.

Massacre
Killing many people, especially if they are defenseless.

Migrant
Someone who chooses to move from one region to another, usually for work.

Native Peoples
The people who first lived in the country/area of the country.

Navajo
The second largest American-Indian tribe, native to the Southwestern states.

Nitroglycerine
A high explosive substance used in the building of railroads.

Outlaw
A criminal.

Panic of 1873
A major financial crash in the United States that led to a six-year depression.

Panning
Sifting for gold, also known as placer mining.

Posse
A group of people gathered up by a sheriff, usually to chase a criminal.

Poverty
Having little money, goods, or means of support.

Prairie
A large area of land with grasses in the Mississippi River valley.

Prospector
Someone hunting for gold.

Rustler
A cattle thief.

Scalping
To slice off the skin on the top of the head as a battle trophy.

Settlers
People seeking new lands.

Sheriff
The main law enforcer in a county.

Sioux
A major American-Indian group of tribes.

Stampede
When a herd of animals begin running with no clear direction or purpose. A large stampede can be dangerous.

Territory
A defined area of land that is considered the possession of a person, state, or country.

Treaty
A written agreement.

Vigilante
A person who takes the law into their own hands by catching and punishing a suspected criminal.

The Major Trails across America's Old West

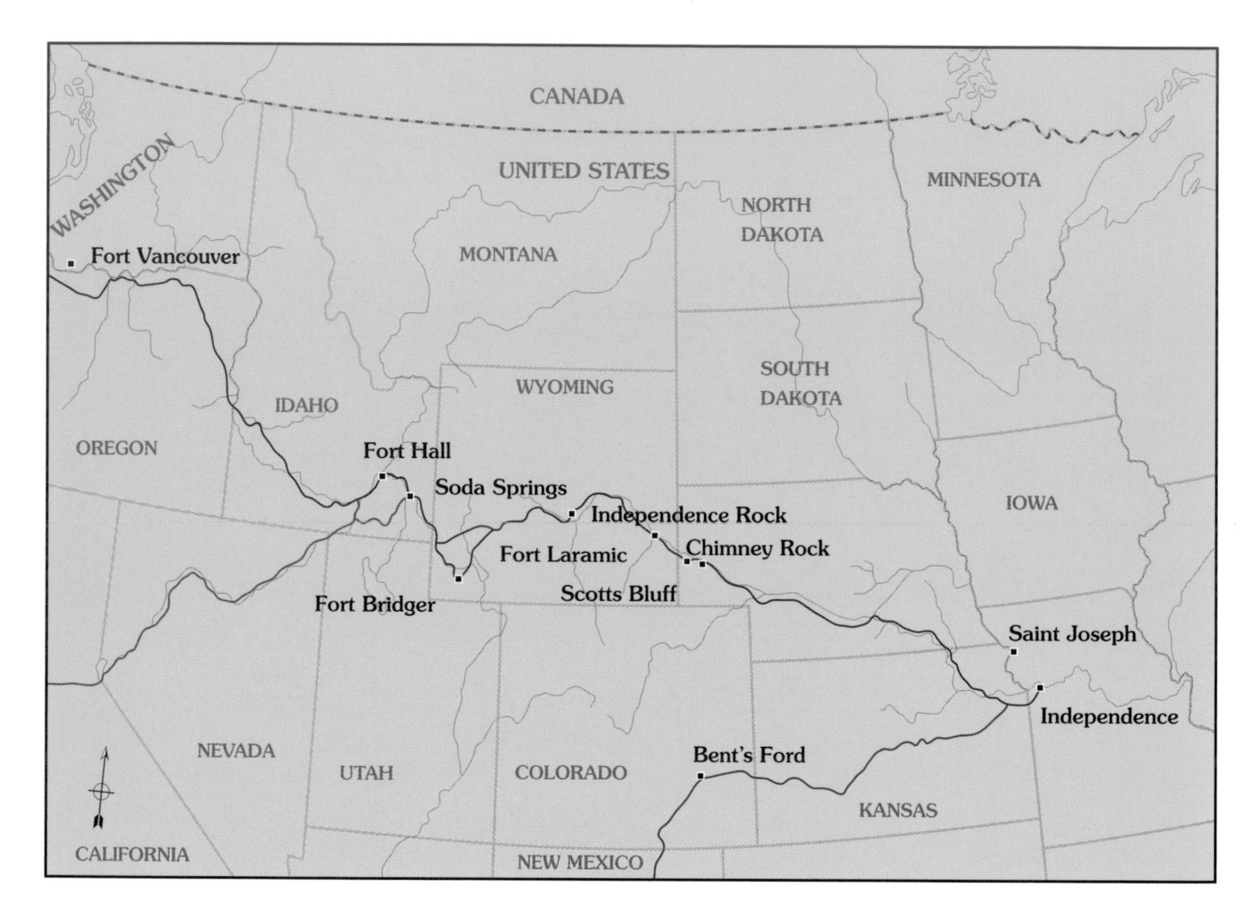

The Oregon Trail, The Santa Fe Trail, and The California Trail were the most frequently used routes across the West. Thousands of people used these routes to seek their riches and start a new life.

SCALE:

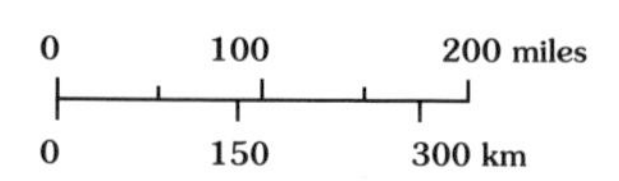

KEY:

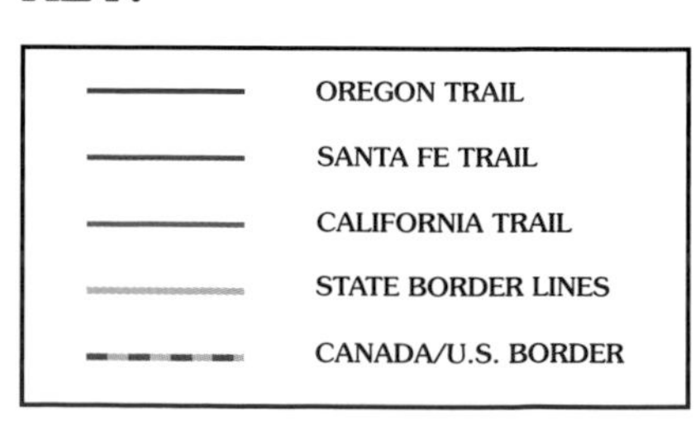

Find Out More

Books

Murray, Stuart. *Wild West* (Eyewitness). New York: DK, 2005.

Wexler, Bruce. *The Wild West Catalog*. New York: Barnes & Noble, 2008.

———. *The Wild, Wild West of Louis L'Amour*. Philadelphia: Running Press, 2005.

Websites

The Heard Museum
www.heard.org/about/index.html

National Cowboy and Western Heritage Museum
www.nationalcowboymuseum.org/info/default.aspx

Nation Oregon/California Trail Center
www.mnsu.edu/emuseum/cultural/northamerica/index.shtml

About the Author

Sean Callery is a children's writer and teacher. He writes on a wide range of subjects including history, science, and the environment. He is also the author of *The Gem Guide to Dictactors*, the history section of the *Kingfisher Explore Encyclopedia,* and he contributed to *The Encyclopedia of Dinosaurs and other Prehistoric Animals*.

Index